HELL
IN
HEAVEN

HELL
IN
HEAVEN

By
Victor A. Arana, M.D.

ARPress
ILLUMINATING IDEAS
EMPOWERING VOICES

ARPress
45 Dan Road Suite 5
Canton MA 02021

Hotline: 1(888) 821-0229
Fax: 1(508) 545-7580

Ordering Information:

Quantity sales. Special discounts are available on quantity purchases by corporations, associations, and others. For details, contact the publisher at the address above.

Printed in the United States of America.

ISBN-13:   Paperback   979-8-89356-302-3
             eBook   979-8-89356-303-0

Library of Congress Control Number: 2024902949

INDEX

Dedicated to my children, Victor A. Arana, JD and Elisa L. Murphy, MBA for inspiring me in my accomplishments.

ACKNOWLEDGEMENTS

I would like to express sincere appreciation to the following:

Jon Murphy,
who created the original and exclusive cover design.

Elisa Murphy,
who coordinated the re-publishing of this book and acts as
my day to day consultant

Diana Rezac,
for her cooperation with the English edition and making the
original publication ready.

Victor A. Arana, J.D.,
who has inspired me to always want more.

ABOUT THE AUTHOR

Victor A. Arana, MD, graduated with high honors in 1961 from San Marcos University School of Medicine, Lima, Peru, the oldest University in America. He was the first and only one among 192 graduates to receive his diploma to practice medicine and surgery in a private ceremony held in the office of the Dean of the Medical School on April 2, 1961.

Victor A. Arana graduating as a Medical Doctor in a Private Ceremony at the office of the Dean of the University of San Marcos, Lima, Peru. By merits, Dr. Arana was the first student graduated in a class of 192.

Dr. Arana then was involved with Dr. Fernando Cabieses Molina, President of the "Universidad del Sur," and Dr. Uladislao Lozano, Principal Professor of Pediatrics at the University of San Marcos, both in Lima, Peru, investigating the oral poliomyelitis vaccine and measles vaccine. He then traveled to the United States to study surgery. Upon his arrival he took the examination requested by the Educational Consul for Foreign Medical Graduates to be recognized as an MD in the US. He performed his internship at Mount Sinai Hospital of Chicago in 1964, and then went to Kansas City, KS, where he performed his junior surgical residency at the University of Kansas Medical Center. After one year in Peru attending to some family problems, he returned to the United States to complete the surgical residency at the University of Nebraska in Lincoln, and Creighton University in Omaha, Nebraska. He also specialized in renal transplantation and urology at Roswell Park Memorial Institute in Buffalo, New York. Dr. Arana published several papers in American and international journals, and he has presented lectures in teaching seminars around the world. He was the first physician involved in the helicopter rescue of highway accidents in 1967 as part of a project "Sky Aid Operation" carried out by the surgical department of the University of Nebraska. This project was later referred to the Department of Defense and the Secretary of the Army of the United States to structure an ongoing program at the national level regarding Air Medical Evacuation System (AMES). Dr. Arana was a member of several American and international organizations. He served as a trustee for the International Academy of Proctology. In 1980 he was the first to publish results of a surgical treatment for the morbidly obese diabetic patient and the results were presented in Rome, Italy, at a seminar of the International Academy of Proctology. Those same results were later presented in New Orleans, LA, in 1981. In the May of 2006 issue of "Contigo Peru in USA," Dr. Arana was recognized as one of the best gastric surgeons in the world. In April of 2007 he published a book, Irregularities in Correctional Institutions. Currently, because of the economical crisis that is mostly affecting the Hispanic population, he is publishing a book, Hell in Heaven, to help immigrants make better decisions when they arrive here. Hopefully, they will better understand this crisis is going to be of a long duration before recovery.

INTRODUCTION

This book is intended for the general Hispanic population to highlight awareness of some of the problems they are likely to encounter when immigrating to the United States of America.

Immigration to this country is mainly by three routes. The most popular is the Mexico-America border, which is used mostly by the illegal immigrants. The majority of the people using this route are Mexicans, Central Americans, and Latin Americans in a lower proportion. Of course, the infiltration of other people promoting terrorism and criminal activity is also using these routes. Before reaching the border of Mexico-America, these people have to face difficulties such as accidents, rapes, violence, abandonment, etc. It is calculated that over 1000 people died in the last four to five years before reaching the Mexico-America border. Once on American soil, they have to face persecution, discrimination, abuse, dangerous encounters in the Arizona desert, etc.

The second route of entrance into the United States is by air. These immigrants comprise individuals with a tourist visa, permanent visa, or American citizenship. This latter group comes from Puerto Rico. Prior todeparture, this group of immigrants preceded their trips by farewell parties and congratulations. Once in the United States, friends or relatives usually welcome them. They enjoy parties and the glamorous times of visiting the wonders of this way of life such as Disney World, Disneyland, Cape Canaveral, etc. After this short period of enjoyment, they wake up in hell. Many of these tourists, especially women, come with the idea of staying in this country, undocumented, with the hope that some time in the future they will obtain citizenship.

A small group of immigrants comes by the third route, namely the water. Mostly these people come from the Caribbean islands, such as Jamaica, Cuba, Dominican Republic, Barbados, etc. Before reaching the shores of the United States, their trip is rough and many do not make it because they are taken into custody by the Coast Guard or die over the water.

The common denominators of problems to the Hispanic immigrants to this country are three.

1. Integration. Hispanics have a difficult time changing the routine life to which they are accustomed, and want to continue with the customs they teach their children in this country. It is difficult to change and adapt to the life of the United States, and they do not learn the laws that need to be observed while living in this country.

2. Language barrier. Hispanics want to preserve their language and culture, which they teach to their children, making communication in this country difficult. Speaking English with a Spanish accent is one of the difficulties in obtaining employment. Of course, one of the biggest difficulties in learning the language is the presence of the television, which presents enjoyable programming in the Spanish language. Hispanics come from work and turn the television on to the Hispanic stations. The governor of California, in one of his speeches, said that instead of watching Spanish programming, immigrants should learn English.

3. Discrimination. It is the law in this country not to discriminate; however, this problem exists. Discrimination is mostly because the Hispanics do not speak or understand the English language. Even the people from Hispanic countries, who feel they have succeeded because of their economic success, have to go through hell to obtain employment. Tohave money does not compensate for the problems one has to go through to reach a good economical position.

This book is being published with the hope that Hispanics will understand the real issues one faces when coming to the United States. We come to heaven; however, we have to live in hell and some of us, including me, will see the light on the other side of the tunnel, but the majority will not.

Sincerely,
Victor A. Arana, MD

CHAPTER 1
TRIP TO USA

As was previously mentioned in the introduction, there are three main modalities of coming to the United States.

The first route is through the Mexican-American border, which is mostly immigration of undocumented individuals. The people who use this modality are mostly Mexicans, a good number of Central Americans, and a few from South America who travel through Mexico to reach the border. This kind of immigrant has their thinking that they are going to find money and comfort on the other side of the border. Guides, also called coyotes, receive a certain amount of money for bringing them, and they bring these immigrants to the border of Mexico with the United States. Some others continue the trip through Arizona, but we will not relate this part of the trip. The trip to the border is very dangerous, and some of them lose the battle. There are rapes and abuse, and even deaths. It is calculated that more than 1000 deaths have been registered in the last 4 to 5 years. Once in the border, they have to face the border patrol. On the other side of the border begins the persecution with a new life of poor living, abuse, low paying jobs and the most difficult for them is that they have to be hiding from persecution by the Immigration officials and in some places by the police department. Summarizing, this trip is very dangerous and many of them do not reach the border of Mexico-United States.

We cannot pass this chapter of persecution without speaking about Sheriff Arpaio of Arizona. He is a good man for Americans but a wanted man by Hispanics.

Actually and honestly he is doing his job. He is tasked with catching undocumented people, and because of the large number of immigrants without documents he has been placing in custody, he has been given nicknames for his actions. Hispanics do not understand that laws govern this country. Any undocumented person who trespasses the borders of the United States becomes a criminal. For Hispanics, criminals are killers of other persons, which is not the interpretation of a criminal by US standards. In any event, this gentleman is actually being harassed by television announcers who perhaps do not understand the laws or conveniently misinterpret them. It is my honest impression that Sheriff Arpaio is only doing the job he is being paid for. Perhaps his modalities of detaining these undocumented persons are somewhat unusual, as well as the incarceration, but one has to assume there is a massive number of immigrants coming through the border, and he has detained more of them than facilities can house.

The second group comes by air, and usually these immigrants have a permanent visa or a tourist visa. A few of them come from Cuba after winning the lottery. In any event, prior to departure, the people who are coming to the United States are congratulated thinking they are coming to a better life. Most of the immigrants who come this route are coming alone or with complete families, as are the ones who are coming from Argentina. I myself flew to the United States and on that flight I found a family of Argentine people, father, mother and three children. In the plane the mother was having vaginal bleeding and she did not know where to go while in Miami. I knew medicine but not the language; however, I was able to conduct them to the hospital and they did a D&C, which made the father, the head of the family, very unhappy because he had to pay a considerable amount of money and that was mostly from the money he brought to stay in this country. In any event, immigrants who come by air usually are congratulated for coming here, as I already mentioned, and also the ones who are working are celebrating farewell parties, organized by coworkers. I can say this is a glorious time for the ones who come with a tourist visa, deciding to stay in the United States. The trip otherwise is a joyful departure, seeing friends at the airport. Once they arrive in the United States, they are welcomed by families, relatives, and mostly friends.

The third group is mostly coming from the Caribbean Islands, and they come by boat. They sometimes come in rudimentary boats and they have to suffer hunger, diseases, and many times even death. They face the Coast Guard before reaching the beaches of the United States. Once in this country, they will have to face all the problems every Hispanic immigrant faces.

Once the Hispanic immigrant is in the United States, they have to face immediate and lifetime problems as will be described later.

CHAPTER 2
WELCOME TO USA

I would like to start this chapter with the words by Dr. Nancy Alvares, (two doctor degrees), to the Hispanic immigrations in the program called "Quien Tiene la Razon?" that means whose fault is it. This is a program presented by Tele Futura from Monday through Friday in which Dr. Alvares is a host. She expressed that at the present time the living expenses in this country are very high for Hispanics, or at least a majority of them, and to undocumented immigrants. She suggested the illegal immigrants go back to their respective countries, get their papers as needed, and then come to this country legally. The reason that I made remarks about the statements of Dr. Alvares is because among the media she is the only one I heard to say the truth. Most of the hosts of similar programs, commentators of television and radio, give false hopes to the illegal immigrations to think that by making them legal that is going to solve their problems. First, I agree with Dr. Alvares because as a physician I was able to see how the Hispanic immigration lives, mainly now that I am working in an area where the majority population is Hispanic.

For immigrants who make it through the Mexico-American border with the aid of coyotes, once they pass the border avoiding the border patrol, they have to face persecution, abuse from the coyotes, and possible incarceration until they get paid. These people, when caught by the Immigration Department, have to go to special places and then they are placed for deportation. If they have families, the case is placed in front of the judge and after they receive a deportation order they usually disobey the orders and become fugitives. The typical, although exaggerated, case was the situation of Elvira Arrellano, who three times ignored the deportation order and as a fugitive took a Christian church as a sanctuary. She made significant political problems and to a certain degree she was the center of attention during immigration meetings asking for the reformation of the immigration laws, claiming she had an American child. Of course, we never knew the father's identity and in the end this problem terminated when she was apprehended during one of the meetings in California and she was sent back to Mexico. In Mexico, she became an activist and she even tried to convince the President of Mexico to become an ambassador of friendship so she could come to the United States. The majority of this immigration group that comes through Mexico-American border remains illegal. They find jobs with false documents and are subject to abuse from the owners of any organization where they work. Other immigrants, especially the ones who come from Cuba, Colombia, or Venezuela, usually try to request refugee visas.

Criminals and terrorists infiltrate into the group that comes through the Mexican-American border. Here, there are also people who have been deported and they return for a second and third time. I know of persons coming for the fourth time with more than one deportation order. Still there is a group of women who come with the idea of becoming pregnant so they will have children born in United States. At this point they request pardons because they have minor children in this country. The group that are not included in this situation, at least a significant number, dedicate to prostitution or work as cleaning ladies or servants, usually abused by their patrons, either with very low salaries or working full time. Furthermore, before they employ these undocumented illegal immigrants, they take their passports and other documents to keep them more secure. Later on, when the employed cleaning ladies or servants request their documents, if they are illegal they do not give them back with the threat that they could go to the Immigration Department and cause their deportation. Of course, there are some of them who have made a complaint and went to court where justice was served ordering these employers to pay for all the time they were sleeping and serving during extra hours and weekends. Of the 1.5 million cleaning personnel, we do not know the actual number in this situation.

The second group that comes by air is mostly people from the middle class. They request tourist visas with the idea of staying in this country. There is a group of travelers with permanent visas and some others without a visa, especially the ones from Argentina and Uruguay. These immigrants usually have relatives or friends who are expecting them and, of course, after arrival they usually enjoy parties and people from their own country willing to take them out for rides or to go to the wonders of this great civilization. Soon after this glorious time, they wake up in hell. They do not have jobs, and they have to work as bartenders in restaurants, and as cleaning ladies. It is estimated that in United States there are about 1.5 million people working as cleaning ladies and maids. The immigrants with permanent visas go on with their life, but usually end close to other persons from their own country. A few of them, physicians and nurses, go and try to take the foreign examination, which is very difficult, and many of them do not pass this examination. Out of necessity they obtain jobs in the hospital as orderlies, labs technicians, or other kinds of nonmedical jobs. In any event, most of these immigrants are looking for survival. They end up in large cities such as Chicago, New York, Los Angeles, Miami, Houston, etc. They may live in communities, mostly in the areas where there are other Spanish-speaking people, mainly Mexicans and blacks, because the real estate in these places is considerably cheaper than in the higher income communities.

The third group that comes by air will have the same problems as the other ones. All depends on the degree of education and the willingness to construct a new future. However, most of them come to live here, to make more money than in their country, which is not enough to have a decent life, but they like to buy cars, televisions and other appliances of modern civilization. Of course, they try to get a credit card, which later on they are unable to pay off.

All of these three groups of immigrants, no matter what their situation, economically or education-wise, all have to face the three major problems: INTEGRATION, LANGUAGE BARRIER AND DISCRIMINATION.

I mentioned Dr. Alvares for her sincerity in telling the truth to future immigrants, not giving false hopes as do the rest of the media, along with the activists. It is difficult to live in this country and I say it here and now, "if I would have to do it again, I would never come here to live in hell in spite that economically I succeeded."

CHAPTER 3
LIVING IN USA

Indeed, we come to this country with expectations we are going to make a lot of money and live with cars, televisions and a big house. We come for the American dream and instead when we wake up we find we had a nightmare. We wake up in hell.

In spite of the illegal immigrants who, from the beginning, have had to live in persecution and abuse by landlords while working for minimal salaries and in very poor conditions and poor hygiene, later survive economically as their living in this country is poorer than in Third World countries.

The most difficult situation the undocumented immigrants face is the apprehension by the Immigration Service. Incidentally, during the last three weeks of the month of September 2008, 1157 undocumented people were taken into custody to see to what group of illegal immigrants they belonged. The majority of detained immigrants came from the area of Los Angeles, and over 400 of them had criminal records. Over 700 had a deportation order with which they did not comply, and the rest of the persons were classified as "miscellaneous." I would like to mention in this chapter the success of a cardiovascular surgeon working in Florida. He was undocumented in this country, who suddenly became a very well known physician. This story does not mention how they became legal. Apparently there were some illegal maneuvers that had to be done to graduate from Harvard University. Recently, there have been more operations taking into custody a good number of illegal immigrants and now they are beginning to mention it could be a racial discrimination as was commented on by a television announcer on 10/1/2008. The case of Sheriff Arpaio has been described, and in spite of being investigated at the request of over a thousand petitions, I feel he is doing his job very well.

The immigrants who come legally also wake up in hell. They came to heaven but the living conditions are not as good as we dreamed. Actually the dream becomes a nightmare for many immigrants. Professionals like me and others reach a good economical situation, but we have to go through the conditions related to integration, language barrier, and discrimination, mostly when we compete with American-born professionals.

However, despite what the activists and media claim in regards to human rights and that we have food on the table because of these cheap labor workers, I would like to make a comment, and this is the truth. This kind of labor work does not pay taxes, and what I see in the medical field is terrible. They do not even have money to pay for a consultation and medications, and worst of all they do not know the English language to exchange dialogue about their conditions with the American doctors.

It is my feeling for what I see Hispanic immigrants live in terrible hygiene conditions as they survive economically. Of course, many of them become members of gangs, others dedicate to crime stealing and trying to cheat the government. As far as the women are concerned, they work as cleaning ladies and servants and have surpassed 1.5 million immigrants. They obtain work in restaurants or turn to prostitution. A group of these women try to get pregnant so they can have children born in the United States and in this way they claim a stay in this country. There have been advertisements for the "sale of human organs," which is against the law in the United States; i.e., a kidney being advertised for $10,000. This is outrageous, and all just to make a living to stay in this country. There are over 500,000 deportation orders of which persons are noncompliant and a few who are smart—they become activists, as in the case of Elvira. Arrellano. Generally, it is my opinion that with the living conditions of the immigrants in this country, except for the ones who succeed economically, it is better to go back to their own countries where they no longer have persecution and can find better jobs, particularly during this economic crisis. However, of course, they will not have cars, credit cards, good streets, televisions and other modern luxuries as are available in this country, even if all these artifacts are obtained with credit that they will never pay. Of all the people who buy televisions on credit cards, 6/10 people have problems paying the balance.

Another significant problem is that Hispanics have begun to buy businesses at inflated prices and, of course, the Hispanic population maintains these businesses. They buy large homes in comparison with standards in other countries, considered to be mansions, paying $300,000 to $350,000 and up. Everything was fine until the economical crisis happened in the United States and at this point they were not able to pay the mortgages for the houses, and they did not buy things as usual with the consequence of losing money in businesses they could not support. The final outcome was losing the businesses and foreclosing the houses. This is the sad situation of not looking towards the future as we think about the good life without measuring the consequences. As a matter of fact, the present economical crisis began with the foreclosure of real estate to Hispanics. The fact is that for the opportunity of having a luxury home, Hispanics were buying real estate at inflated prices. The facilities, even by banks, to possess real estate without high-dollar down payments and sometimes very low monthly payments, prompted this crisis. People were not able to pay, even taking credit cards to meet the payments for the houses in which they lived. Foreclosure of a few million homes in the United States was the beginning of this economical crisis.

A similar situation is still happening. The advertisement of the car dealers has a lot to do with this problem as they usually say, "you come in walking and you will leave driving." You do not need to be a citizen, you don't need to have documents, you don't need a driver's license, and we will secure the financing of your car. Sometimes you do not even have to make a down payment. In that way, many Hispanics and other people in the same category are buying cars without knowing later on they would not be able to make the monthly payments. Now, the next step is going to be repossession of the car, which is going to add to the economical crises in spite of the bail out of the $700 billion.

As a matter of comment, the present economical crisis will probably last for a few years. Now that the United States has a new president, a minority himself, it is my impression he is not going to solve the economical crisis in a short time. On the other hand, the promises he made to minorities, especially Hispanics, about migratory reform will not happen because he has to secure the borders south and north before he can make reform. Moreover, he is not going to be able to legalize about 15 million illegal Hispanics to become legal citizens because, in a sense, that will discredit him as this is against the law. As you know, first he promised he was going to give reform in the first 100 days. Later on, he said a year. If it ever happens, it will be with restrictions where about 10 to 15% of this population will be eligible for citizenship. This comment is directed towards the Hispanics who have some money in savings. They would be better off to return to their country and start a new life there. If they do not have any savings, they will be better off asking for help from their relatives. Those in debt who do not want to return to their country have to make the decision to live in this humiliation asking for food stamps, help from the government, living in terrible conditions, or taking jobs above described, being abused by their landlords.

On the other hand, I can tell you stories that will probably amaze you about how these problems are being coped with one by one. I myself was subjected to abuse and peer discrimination, as I will describe when I relate my autobiography. The economical status we attain by going through all these problems, myself being a physician, do not compensate for all the trials and tribulations one has to endure. Recently I experienced the unbelievable abuse of a Hispanic from a Hispanic that I will relate when I describe my autobiography.

CHAPTER 4
INTEGRATION

Integration is one of the most difficult tasks for a Hispanic immigrant.

Hispanics come to this country not to integrate to the new culture. The majority of immigrants will not change, especially Mexicans, who comprise the majority of immigrants. They always say that they are Mexicans until they die, and also the first generation of these immigrants claim publicly they were born on this soil, but they are Mexicans and they will be Mexicans first. Now comes the major problem that most of the immigrants who are here illegally, and many of the legal ones, are not the most educated people. They come because they want to be supported by this country. The rich people do not come to this country because they feel their money is going to be integrated with the American economy, and then they have to pay taxes everywhere.

My personal experience is that they will never integrate, they never will become defenders and supporters of this country. A few people go into the Armed Forces because they are pursuing residence and citizenship to be comfortable in this country. There will be a few who are feeling different, but this is a great minority.

If we consider minorities, we can see that the blacks are integrated to this country. The example is how the redemption basketball team USA played in Beijing with the heart to defend the United States of America. On the one hand, white people supported them without any difference despite the fact the redemption team USA was only composed of black players; the only white person was the coach.

The election of President Barack Obama is an example that once one has immigrated to this country and follow the rules and laws of this country, there is not any more obvious discrimination. He is now president for four, and perhaps eight, years. However, I doubt that will happen. Being a minority himself, I do not think he will comply with all the promises he made, especially to Hispanics.

In regards to the election of Barack Obama, he immigrated to the country, was a Senator, and in years to come the United States of America will show to the world that there is not any more discrimination in this country, though not true in certain cases. I will describe more about President Obama in the chapter of discrimination.

What is more, it is difficult to understand how people in the media, Hispanic radio and television, encourage the immigrants to bring their cultures, not to change, and to defend their countries of origin. I was listening to one of the shows called, Rocio, and I heard how the host, Rocio Sanchez, was actually trying to emphasize how the food we eat is the product of the work of the immigrants, which is true, but many of these immigrants do not pay taxes.

In my practice, I have seen where the tax money is going in relation to the Hispanic immigration. There are patients requesting disability with 6 to 7 children, and these patients are middle aged. There are other patients who are brought by their children and relatives because they are sick, and they practically go from the plane to the hospitals. The social workers tell them not to worry about the payments because there is a Federal fund to pay the bills, which is our tax money. Some people have a card allowing them free care in emergency rooms. They abuse the system, overloading the work of the emergency room physicians and staff, with the consequence of shortage of physicians, which lowers the quality of work in what is a proper response to medicine.

In any event, besides using all those services and abuse of the American system, claiming human rights, I do not think they feel guilty when they request those services because they know they are practically begging for something they do not deserve. To obtain medical services and other programs such as money to live on, Medicaid, and food stamps, develops the sense of humiliation. Incidentally, there is a publication detailing the cost of the illegal immigration to the economy worsening the present economical crisis.

Once more I would like to refresh the words of Dr. Nancy Alvares who plainly expresses her thoughts about living in this country. Of course, the media and the activists encourage this Hispanic immigration to blackmail the candidates for the presidency of the United States, exchanging the vote for an immigration reform that will enclose the legality of the illegal immigrations. Instead, the media and the television should warn the new immigrants to be aware of the abuse they are subject to as it was previously discussed. In any event, knowledge about what is going on, especially in the areas where Hispanics are located, should cut off the number of abuses that mainly women are subjected to.

CHAPTER 5
LANGUAGE BARRIERS

This is a difficult subject for Hispanic immigrants. The majority of immigrants who come from Latin American countries do not speak or understand English at all. When they arrive they usually go to places where they do not have the pressure to learn English, as in areas where only Spanish is spoken. These cities are mainly New York, Washington DC, Chicago, Miami, Houston, Los Angeles, etc., where the majority of the population is immigrants of Spanish origin and even the current mayor, from Los Angeles, is Spanish. Therefore, they find jobs where they do not have to speak English and, of course, they do not have better jobs. As was previously related, they are waitresses in restaurants owned by Hispanics. They work in household jobs where their employers abuse them. The other kinds of jobs they find are in crime or prostitution.

In Los Angeles, there is a street where prostitutes look for their customers. This is Sepulveda Street where prostitution runs in view of everyone, and there are no police to avoid this kind of illegal activity.

Hispanics usually come from work and the first thing they do is place the television on Telemundo, Univision, Telefutura, etc. In these channels they present programs that are very attractive for this group of immigrants, especially given the high quality of pictures and the facility to buy a television. I am not aware of any course of Spanish being presented on these televisions, but on the contrary they have media that encourages immigrants to stay in this country, especially illegal immigration, releasing false expectations. After 40 years in this country, when I stay at home for two days watching these television stations, my English becomes a little bit distorted and difficult to understand. You can imagine how it would be for people who do not know English; they see all these programs, not only adults but children as well. They all say that one person is worth two when they know two languages; perhaps this doesn't apply to this country. As they say, the person who speaks three languages is trilingual, the person who speaks two languages bilingual, and the person who speaks only one language is an American. Poor jobs, abuse, and exploitation of the Hispanic immigration by their own people is not uncommon. On the other hand, because of the poor knowledge of the language, Hispanics cannot obtain good jobs in American companies.

It is important for the immigrants from Spanish countries to know they will never learn to speak English like an American. Therefore, I would advise them to teach the new generations to speak English first, and perhaps later on they can learn Spanish, even if they speak this language with an American accent, which is more important than to speak English with a Spanish accent. In summary, it is apparent now that discrimination, due to language, is more important than due to the name. Perhaps in the year 2050 when the Spanish immigration becomes larger than the American population, they will change the laws and make Spanish an official language of the United States of America. However, now we have to speak English as Americans do, and overall we need to know how to write this new language that is very difficult to learn. Another important point is that we should look back to the time when we went to high school and Spanish- speaking people taught English for five years. At the end of high school, very few students can put a sentence together in English. A few of them who have good economical resources send their children to school where they study in English. There are very few of these expensive schools and usually these people with good economical situations rarely come to the United States as a permanent immigrant. It is a shame to spend five years learning English in high school knowing this is an official course and at the end of the fifth year we do not have even the principles of English or American language. The English language is very difficult to learn.

CHAPTER 6
DISCRIMINATION

Race discrimination is more frequently due to the illegal immigration from the developing countries to the developed countries. A large number of illegal immigrants are immigrating to countries such as Germany, Italy, Spain, and Japan and massively to the United States. However, the word discrimination has been used and abused by Hispanics as a mechanism of defense with purpose. True discrimination exists, but is a rare occurrence. However, we have become paranoid because of what we see in the media and in the previous immigrants. Publicized cases of discrimination will be discussed.

Especially the media, as hate against Americans, described the case of Ramirez who was beaten by three American youngsters. At this time, these three aggressors are indicted but not convicted. It is my impression that knowing how Hispanics, especially Mexicans, react to some insults, there was a provocation and, of course, the results were not good.

A very publicized incident happened during a meeting held by Hispanics last year, in California and was, of course, labeled a true case of discrimination. It is my observation that this kind of incident happens when the police department intervenes. I have seen similar cases in other countries where the socalled "abuse of the security forces in correctional institutions and police" were actually cases of insurrections. Blaming these cases on discrimination is a job that the media wants to create to entertain the audience, who is mostly Hispanic, especially by the Hispanic television.

True discrimination exists, but as I previously mentioned, a rare occurrence. What I experienced while I was working at Methodist Medical Center, St. Joseph, MO, in 1980, was a case of true discrimination, but later on the insurance company and the attorneys who initiated the situation vindicated me. In any event, the chief of surgery, Dr. Richard Craig, was asked to write a letter of recommendation and in his letter directed to me he stated the following.

"Dr. Arana cannot be recommended because he is foreign born and foreign trained…."

We come to this country with the paranoid idea that we are being discriminated against for everything. For example, when we apply for a job for which we believe we are qualified, but the job is given to an American, we believed we have been the targets of discrimination. What we usually sense is the feeling of what we call "pronoia," which is different from paranoia. Pronoia is a term given to the persons who believe they are better than what they really are. This situation is very common in Hispanics as they are always on the defensive side when they make errors.

CHAPTER 7
MY OWN EXPERIENCE IN USA

I arrived in this country on March 13, 1963, which was a Sunday morning. I then went to downtown Miami to look for the Greyhound as recommended by my mentor, Dr. Lozano, Professor of Pediatrics at the University of San Marcos, oldest university in America. I remember we left Miami at around 5:00 p.m. and then started the long journey to Kansas City, MO. While near Tennessee, I saw a man of dark complexion, and I asked him if he was Spanish, or if he spoke Spanish. He replied he knew Spanish, but was an Indian from Tennessee. I asked him to take me to eat and, of course, at this time I was really hungry as the night before I did not have

The Frederick Hotel, located in downtown, Kansas City, Missouri. It was the first stop for Dr. Arana upon his arrival to the United States.

any food because of the language barrier. In any event, we traveled for about a day until he told me that the next was his last stop because he reached his end point of his trip. We went to the cafeteria and filled up my pockets with sandwiches for the rest of the trip as he told me the trip would take probably another day. In any event, we arrived in Kansas City at about 7:00 p.m. on March 16, and at that time, after I took my luggage, I asked for a taxicab to take me to a good hotel. Of course, I did not know how I pronounced "good hotel" in English. He went around the corner and took me to a hotel called, "Frederick Hotel," and there was a sign that said $2.00 to $2.50 and up. Since

I did not know anything else, I just went to my room. I began to call all the Spanish names in the telephone book until the letter C. At this point I found the name of Michael Edward Castillo. Dr. Castillo answered the telephone. At that time I asked him if he knew how to speak Spanish. Coincidentally, after we met together, I found out Dr. Castillo was my teacher while at the International Petroleum Company in Talara, Peru, where I performed my internship and he was now an ophthalmologist. In any event we visited for about 15 minutes until he asked me where I was staying. At this point he told me not to get out of my room, that he was coming right away as there were concerns regarding the general location of the hotel and the surrounding area. It was on Wednesday evening. He took all the money I brought with me, $3000. He left $50.00 with me and told me he was coming on the following Sunday to take me to lunch in his home. Not knowing where to go there was a store by the corner called Park View stores. I went in and bought a case of Coca-Cola and a large bag of potato chips. For the next three days my meals were potato chips and Coca- Cola. I was studying for my foreign examination required for recognition of my medical doctor degree from Peru. On the following Sunday, Dr. Castillo appeared to take me to his home to eat. When I arrived, I saw a good piece of roast beef in the center of the dining table. You can imagine how excited I was. I ate as you cannot imagine, and when I went home I realized I was having diarrhea. The diarrhea lasted for about a day and Dr. Castillo then provided some medication, which was very effective. My next appointment with the Director of Medical Education at St. Joseph Hospital in Kansas City, MO was on Wednesday. The above story was published by the Jackson Independence of Jonesboro, LA, in the year 1972, "The Story of the Potato Chips." This type of situation in which we had to suffer as I did tells us how much we have to go through in this country.

Another story to follow the above was one of abuse of authority. After I had my appointment with the Director of Medical Education, I was placed to work as an assistant surgeon in the operating room at St. Joseph Hospital in Kansas City, MO. After three months of working, I used to see Sr. Martha Frances, who was the head of the operating room, giving everyone their pay envelopes with their checks. No check for me. I could not speak too much English; however, I was very good helping in the operating room with the doctors who needed my assistance. After three months, Dr. Carlos Santoro, from Puerto Rico, decided to help after I told him the situation. He went to see the administrator of the hospital, who was Sr. Thomas Acquinas, and her reply to Dr. Santoro was, "Dr. Santoro, this is not your business. If Dr. Arana wants money, he has to come and talk to me." Anyway, after that episode I decided not to go to work, acting as a "real peruvian," and the following, Monday I stayed in my apartment, which was across the street from the hospital. Sr. Martha Frances called me and asked me why I did not report to work, and I replied to her, "no money, no work." She came to see me in the apartment and asked me to go to work, and she was going to be responsible for my paycheck. Indeed, I began to receive my checks, but did not receive the previous three months of back pay. Well, that probably was my contribution to St. Thomas Aquinas. As soon as I passed my test to recognize my medical degree in this country I decided not to work there any more, acting again as a "real peruvian," and I went to work at North Kansas City Memorial Hospital as a surgeon's assistant. Previously, I was making $250/month and, of course, at this new hospital they began paying me $800/month, which was a big difference. This is the kind of abuse we have to go through for being in this country. Once more, I would like to say I came to heaven, but when I woke up I was in hell.

I went to perform my internship at Mt. Sinai Hospital in Chicago, Illinois, where all the interns and most of the residents were foreigners. However, the majority, perhaps 99% of the persons in training, were Jewish. They used to tease me I had the nose of a Jewish person, but since I was not Jewish, maybe that was the reason they got confused and accepted me. My internship went through without significant problems. Of course, I was at the level of the residents. Before I finished my internship, a doctor with a good reputation, the Director of Medical Education, asked me if I wanted to stay for my residency, but it was a pyramidal system that began the first year with five residents, and we finish with only two, so they were eliminating residents during the next years. Since I was not Jewish, I decided to come back to Kansas City, MO. I was accepted at the University of Kansas Medical Center where I performed my junior year of surgical training. In this hospital, I met one of the leading thoracic surgeons in the world who writes in the famous surgical book of Lewis, which is composed of 12 volumes. The name of the surgeon who was the chief of the department of surgery was Frank F. Albritten. My salary was $250/month and I had no other income. Some of the residents who were Americans used to moonlight working in other hospitals as night emergency room physicians. At the end of the year I decided to go to Nashville, Tennessee to St. Thomas Hospital affiliated with Vanderbilt University, but then my father became sick and I returned to Peru. Once my father recovered, I decided to go back and here began my good luck, if I call this situation good luck. I came to a Veterans Administration Hospital in Lincoln, NE, affiliated with the University of Nebraska, and I met the great surgeon, Steve Carveth, who was at that time putting together the CPR method, mostly known all over the world as Cardiopulmonary Resuscitation. How lucky I was! Not only did I meet Dr. Steve Carveth, but also I met a very bright, beautiful employee of the Veterans Administration. As soon as I saw her, even without inviting her to go out, I thought, "This lady is going to be the mother of my children." She was the daughter of a German mother, and had a cousin who was a physician. After I finished my residency under the University of Nebraska and Creighton University also of Nebraska, I decided to go learn kidney transplantation and urology, so I applied to the largest cancer hospital located in Buffalo, New York, Roswell Park Memorial Institute. Here at Roswell Park, I met the great Dr. Gerald P. Murphy, better known as GP Murphy. This doctor was the key for the performance of the heart transplant in South Africa, and later he was the director of the popular Cancer Journal for Clinicians, the official journal of the American Cancer Society. I married the woman from the Nebraska Veterans Administration Hospital, and I decided to come back to Lincoln, Nebraska, as I liked the Midwest surrounded by mostly American people. There were a few Mexicans who came to work with the railroad and here was the real American life. When working as a chief resident of the Veterans Administration Hospital and

St. Elizabeth Community Health Center, my son was born. At this time I realized I did not have money to pay for the delivery, and I had to pay with my credit card, like many Spanish people do. This was my second wake-up and then I decided to look for money.

While I was in Lincoln, Nebraska, I participated in the first helicopter rescue in 1967 as part of a program, Sky Aid Operation, that was under the surgical department of the University of Nebraska. The first rescue was during a cold night with ice on the ground on Interstate 80 after an accident. As a doctor, I put my crew together after a helicopter from the Air Force came to go with us, and the rescue was a success. This operation was then referred to the Department of Defense who later designated a captain in the Army to study the feasibility of this operation for civilian rescue. This is how the helicopters became a part of the medical profession.

During the time I came back to Peru in the year 1966, I found a good friend, Dr. Segundo Roncal, from Trujillo. We became good friends and we kept in contact from time to time. At this time we had the idea to work together. We established a joint practice in Jonesboro, LA where we founded the first kidney transplant program in mid-Louisiana. We were the only ones with a dialysis program outside the Ochsner Clinic, New Orleans, and Shreveport, LA. We were serving the rural areas. During this time I was able to afford a beautiful house with a swimming pool. During this time my daughter was born. I decided to leave Jonesboro mostly because of the amount of minorities in this area. I liked the American life, and I looked for several places until I decided to reestablish my life in St. Joseph, MO in 1974. By this time I was already a trustee for the

International Academy of Proctology, and during this period of time I published about 15 papers in American and international journals and presented seminars around the world. I was discriminated in the places where I used to practice; however, there was not anything I could prove. I was paranoid until 1984 when I was sued for a malpractice medical condition. It clearly stated that I was not at fault; however, a recommendation letter requested of Dr. Richard Craig, Chief of Surgery of the hospital where this case was performed, clearly disclosed a sense of discrimination. In any case, for the knowledge of the reader, I would like to state that I initiated a countersuit against the insurance company, one of the largest in the world, Medical Protective, and I was vindicated by the insurance company and by the attorneys who took the letter of Dr. Richard Craig to settle the case. This letter served for settlement of the case, in one of its paragraph stated, "Dr. Arana cannot be recommended because he is foreign born and foreign trained..." This letter was a clear proof that there is discrimination, mainly when we establish competition. I was one of the leading surgeons in this medical center and a good friend of one of the best pathologists in the world, Dr. Thomas Sodoman, and Dr. Carlos Moya. In this town of St. Joseph, MO I built a house that was completely unusual and very beautiful giving the impression of a resort. My children practically grew up in St. Joseph, MO, in this particular house.

Private residence of Dr. Arana in Saint Joseph, Missouri,
United States of America

During the first few days of my official retirement I began
to watch television, and I became fascinated and practically
addicted to the history of the Midwest. Of course, while in
St. Joseph, MO, I knew about Jesse James and the James'
brothers. I also was aware of the first mail system that
used to leave from St. Joseph, the Pony Express. Later
on came the trains that departed from Omaha, NE, and as
the song says, "goes through Atchison, Topeka, KS, Sante
Fe, New Mexico" and from there to San Francisco with
the famous Frisco train.. I studied the life of the Midwest
and, of course, my attention was to Wyatt Earp and his

fight with the Clanton family in Tombstone, AZ at the famous OK Corral. Not last were the Dalton brothers who ended in Coffeyville, KS. I came to Coffeyville looking for the Dalton Brothers. I was somewhat depressed and feeling lonely. Then, an unbelievable dream happened. I walked into doctors' clinic and surprisingly, in spite of this old building, my first impression was the contrast of its contents. There was a group of pretty faces showing like red and yellow roses lost upon the old wrinkled faces of elderly people. Roses with only two thorns. After I toured the place, I came out of the building and five hours later I woke up in my condo in Treasure Island, FL, exclaiming, "I was dreaming." I just saw such a contrast between the beauty and the ugly with only two thorns, and a check for $5,000. My daughter then told me, "Dad, you were not dreaming. The beautiful roses were the girls working in Jerry's place, the wrinkled faces were the old patients, and the two thorns were Jerry, the owner, and Jack, Jerry's assistant.

At this point I found a position as a surgeon in one of the groups operating in Coffeyville, KS. While in this community, there was another group that acted as a rival directed by an Indian, Dr. Sanduh. After he saw my work, mainly in major surgery and endoscopy, he became aware that he was not able to compete with me. However, what decided for him to fight directly against me was in the celebration of Doctors' Day. There was a party celebrated at the country club of Coffeyville, KS. The majority of physicians were older physicians who attended this party with their wives of the same age. Of course, I wanted to be the talk of the party and to call attention I decided to go to this party with a friend of mine whom two years before represented Coffeyville, KS as Miss Coffeyville. Of course, when we showed to the party there was total surprise. This young lady was dressed attractively. Of course I was with white suite, white shirt, white shoes and a red tie. From here on Dr. Sanduh developed a jealousy against me, both medically and personally and became my enemy. I was not ready to fight again, and I decided to peacefully go back to Treasure Island, FL and to continue my retirement life. This is a clear case of discrimination and, of course, Dr. Sanduh was a powerful man as he donated a radiation therapy machine to this hospital. However, this discrimination was not by an American person, but by an Indian person, which means competition is part of discrimination wherever we go in this world.

I decided to leave Coffeyville because Jerry, the physician/cardiologist, was under investigation for malpractice and for performing unusual procedures in his office. Eventually, Dr. Jerry was suspended from the medical staff, and of course, the ones working for him, including myself, were not welcome in the community. Again, back to Treasure Island.

I, myself, think that I succeeded in regards to my practice of surgery and my life was apparently good with good economical condition, raising two beautiful and educated children, and anyone can place me at the level of Hispanics who succeeded in this country. However, to live within a group of physicians who discriminated against me because of the competition was not good. I was in hell in spite that the place was heaven.

Thinking back, I believe if I was in a good environment my skills in surgery probably were better. During the time I was in St. Joseph, MO, I took care of my nephew who went to school as a senior in high school and despite being the only foreigner he was never discriminated against. The reason was because he was not competing with anyone and, of course, he was the relative of a surgeon. This is a clear example that we abuse the term discrimination, but most of the time we are paranoid thinking that everywhere, every time we are set aside because of being a minority coming from a Hispanic country. The remainder of my time in St. Joseph was the same with hostility on the part of the American physicians. There were a few foreigners, but I was the only foreign surgeon active in the practice of medicine. At the age of 62, I decided to quit doing surgery and at the graduation of my daughter I decided to move to Florida as my son played tennis for the University of Missouri at Kansas City, and my daughter played tennis for Creighton University of Omaha, NE. I thought they wanted to continue playing tennis and that was the reason I moved to Florida. The mother of the children moved to Austin, TX, and she was very successful in what she was doing, reaching national achievements. I am 75 years old and I am working in a territory that is mostly composed of Hispanic immigrants. Most of them are at the poor level living in terrible conditions, not having a good economical situation, not even enough to meet their everyday needs. I, myself, decided to do general practice at this point to help the Hispanic immigrants, and as the economical situation in this area is very poor, most of the time I donate my services. However, I feel sorry and sad seeing Hispanics coming to this country to live in this humiliation and worse off than they were in their native country. To practice general medicine, I trained myself for a few months with a foreign physician, Dr. Eugenia Seidel, in a state office, and later on I went to work at the Department of Corrections for the State of Florida for 16 months. At the end of my employment at the Department of Corrections, I was able to publish a book entitled, "Irregularities in Correctional Institutions" and in that book I described how poor the medicine is in this state, at least in the state correctional facilities.

Recently, I went to work in South Florida at two urgent care clinics . I found out quickly that these clinics, which are owned by Hispanics, exploit illegal immigrants and the poor, and their main purpose is making money, no matter what it takes. This way to make money also takes advantage of the country by engaging in illegal practice methods with the sick immigrants, employing methods that fill their pockets with money. More details will be in the chapter of health issues.

To end this chapter, I would like to mention that in my free time I help my country of origin. I reconstructed a church in a resort area of Peru; I have a soccer team in the first division of the area of the city of Trujillo, Peru, where I was born. I am the protagonist of the celebration of the city patron of Trujillo. I organized national competition in tennis. I am one of the fathers of chess. Because of Dr. Fidel Alvarado and others, we made this a part of the high school curricula to increase the ability of the students to resolve new problems, thereby improving their intelligence. I helped my country and continue doing it. This help is with my money, which speaks for the love of my people. My "creed" is love your neighbor as you love yourself.

The bottom line is the question, is it worth a Peruvian who finished medical school at the top in his class leaving his relatives, his family, his roots, his friends, to come to the United States to encounter these problems? The answer is – if I have to do it again, I would not emigrate out of my country. The economical situation that I have I could have in my country. However, when I decided to be American and took the oath of citizenship on May 2, 1973, my child's birthday, I integrated to this country and I feel I am an American. I am happy there are minority successes, such as the famous redemption team USA representing the United States in basketball at the Beijing Olympics. The team was composed only of black athletes who presented with American names, such as Labron James, Koby Bryant, Jason Kidd, etc., but in talking to the media they made it very clear they were defending the great country of the United States.

On January 20, 2009, Barack Obama took the oath as president of United States, which ends the discriminatory concept. Now, we have made history in the developed countries by electing an African-American president.

CHAPTER 8
HEALTH ISSUES AND CONCERNS

Undoubtedly, health issues destabilize the economy of Hispanic immigrants who do not have health insurance and, of course, the most affected immigrants are those who are undocumented. We are going to discuss some of the health issues that create a problem not only for the patients, but also for the doctors attending to their problems.

The silent killer – heart attacks – usually places the patients at the side of the disabled. Many of them looks for evaluation for disability and from this time on they become a taxpayer burden. On the other hand, with disability the living conditions become poor. However, there is good news and bad news. The good news is that this kind of condition, coronary thrombosis, can be prevented. The bad news is that to diagnose the preventable condition, the best care is not within reach of many immigrants.

The patient comes to see a doctor at the age when most of these so- called heart attacks occur. There are two tests that can predict the rate of occurrence of coronary thrombosis, a treadmill test and coronary CT scan. When the patient comes asymptomatic but is obese, has diabetes, high blood pressure, or high cholesterol, we suspect coronary thrombosis will be the next problem, and a treadmill test or coronary CT scan becomes part of the required testing. Prescriptions are then given to the patients, but they usually do not comply with the medication regimen because of lack of funds to pay for the medications, and the subsequent follow-up testing.

Obesity and diabetes, type 2, are preconditions to coronary

artery disease. Unfortunately, obesity presents mostly in Hispanics. For some reason, there is a high number of overweight patients and many reach morbid obesity. Many of these patients become diabetic and they develop the microvascular and macrovascular complications of diabetes such as hypertension, renal failure, or diabetic retinopathy, conditions that need consistent monitoring, but this cannot be done in an immigrant population because of financial considerations. It is almost impossible to successfully counsel a Hispanic to lose weight. They do not exercise. The obesity becomes more and more pronounced until one day we diagnose elevated blood sugar, hypertension, or other co morbid conditions. Unfortunately, the incidence of obesity and hypertension is higher within the Hispanic population in the United States. The recommendation to undergo gastric bypass surgery, especially in the morbidly obese patient, is not possible because it is costly and even prohibitive from an economical point of view within the majority of the Hispanic population.

Speaking about medical expenses, I would like the reader to know, and perhaps also the activists and people in the media, what I saw recently when I went to work in South Florida. The exploitation of Hispanic immigrants by others of the same race is incredible. I saw abuse, and even harm, to some of the patients, mostly because the practice of medicine is being done by physician assistants who are directed to make money without the direct supervision of a medical doctor. I cannot believe physicians are supervising these physician assistants because the few medical histories I reviewed give the impression this kind of practice is mostly with the idea of increasing revenues for the clinic, and in this way maintaining a good income for their existence. About 2-1/2 weeks was sufficient for me to realize this practice probably contributes to destabilizing the immigrants who work to survive in this economical crisis. I do not want to go into details because it may compromise the persons for whom I worked.

While working at Methodist Medical Center in St. Joseph, and before 1980, I began a prospective study to treat morbidly obese diabetic patients by gastroplasty. I performed surgery in diabetic patients who were over 100 pounds above ideal weight. The results of this study were gratifying, and I presented my report at the seminar of the International Academy of Proctology held in Rome in 1980, and a year later I presented this report in New Orleans, LA. As I mentioned, the results were gratifying, mainly because postoperative follow-up was done by myself and not the referring physician. Currently, I am trying to develop a weight loss program.

HIV and hepatitis C. These two deadly conditions have a higher incidence in the Hispanic populations in the United States. Perhaps the promiscuity and unprotected sex within the Hispanic community make these problems more frequent. These generally end in complications that cannot be treated because of ignorance, especially as far as hepatitis C is concerned, and the lack of comfortable economic situation.

Elective surgeries within the Spanish population are almost impossible unless they have health insurance. Presently, with the economic crisis, it is more difficult to treat people with mild symptoms who present with conditions requiring surgery, such as cholecystectomy, repair of hernias, etc.

Special procedures and miscellaneous: Patients who

need annual check- ups for breast mammograms and pelvic examination with Pap smear miss many conditions because of their economical situation. Colonoscopy or upper endoscopy to diagnose GI bleeding or abdominal pain often does not happen because of finances. I can continue on and on presenting medical practices that are very frustrating because we cannot do a proper work-up to diagnose and treat these patients. They come back to the office because they need medication refills for chronic conditions such as high blood pressure.

In my current practice in an area where the majority is of Hispanic descent, it is very difficult for me to practice medicine when I do not have the proper tools for diagnosis and treatment. It is frustrating when patients do not follow the recommendations or indications for special procedures, and I have to write an additional note to protect myself from malpractice explaining the patient was again asked to have these procedures done, but they were not proceeding because of lack of funds. My frustration is getting to the point that, while I am trying to help the Hispanic population with the language barrier, I am almost ready to quit the practice of medicine.

In this chapter I have to mention a group of immigrants who are being brought by their children who are legal residents. They practically come from the plane to the hospital to be treated for free with Federal funds and then they face the problem of follow-up. Those patients remain in this country going in and out of the emergency room because in that way they will not have to pay for services. However, they crowd the emergency rooms decreasing the efficiency of the emergency room physicians, which is another problem created by this type of immigrant. It is my recommendation that these latter patients will be better treated in their own countries where specialization of medicine is like here in this country. On the other hand, they will not leave behind their friends, their roots and overall they will not have the hassle of the language.

One of the important subjects about this chapter is vaccination. I am not going to speak about the vaccination in children, but it is important to discuss the vaccination of adolescents with the vaccine for prevention of the hepatitis and the human papilloma virus, or HPV. During the last week in my practice, I saw three patients, white women born in United States. One was 15 years old, the second was 19 years old and the third one was 21 years old. They came for physical examinations. They had not received a vaccination related to the development of these conditions. They knew about these vaccinations but they did not receive the medicine, and we are discussing patients born in United States to Hispanic parents.

COMMENTS

This manuscript has been written to educate and make aware the future and present immigrants regarding the problems they can encounter when coming to live in a developed country without knowing laws, cost of living, and other situations that we are not accustomed to having in third world countries. This message is mainly for the Hispanics or any person who is planning to come to the US, principally residents of predominantly Hispanic countries who are already suffering the consequences of the same high cost of living that we encounter in a developed country, the group who come legally, and the ones who from the beginning are illegal aliens, but come with the idea of staying in this country.

Before I discuss some of the obstacles I would like to discuss two fairly typical points for all the immigrants; the medical problems they may encounter during their life in this country and a second point, so well publicized by the Hispanic media, the separation of the family when the parents of American children are subject to deportation.

As far as the medical problems, I agree that there are too many uninsured patients in the United States living here each day that they might get sick or injured. When they do, they often do not see the doctor until it is too late, said Nancy Nielson, MD, President of the American Medical Association. We have to be practical and state that most of the uninsured people in this country are of Hispanic origin living in poor conditions and, of course, the great number are illegal immigrants. I see no theoretical solvency, especially for the illegal Hispanic immigrants. My appreciation in my practice is that these people who do not have insurance crowd the emergency rooms where they do not have to pay because of grants from the Federal government. This makes the work of the emergency room personnel greater giving a poor evaluation of the patient. Perhaps President Obama will include illegal Hispanics in his general health insurance.

A second sore point that is well publicized by the media, especially on television, is separation of the family. The case of Elvira Arelano has been described already, and she ended up being deported and eventually the child followed her. What causes an alert is the deceiving discussions of very important persons. In the case of the conductor of the program, Caso Cerrado (Closed Case), Ana Maria Polo was encouraging the family that was deported to her country. On the telephone, the mother who is already deported, was really claiming her three daughters, 13, 8 and 5 years of age, and this attorney was persuading the mother to leave the three daughters with a friend of a poor economical situation. The father of the three daughters was in the courtroom and he was also going to his country because of a deportation notice, but he wanted to take the three daughters.

The case that was discussed mostly was the separation of the family, but I think the law is the law, and this is the first time I see an attorney going against the law. The 13-year-old daughter was not born in this country. Now my question is, who is separating the family? It is obvious that the illegal immigrants come knowing that some day they are going to be deported if they are caught. Many of them come through the border to get pregnant with the idea that perhaps having a child born in the United States will grant them a visa. It was my surprise that the representative, Luis Rodriguez, was interfering with the deportation of a mother because she was leaving her children. Unfortunately, this mother of three children got married with a resident of Chicago, but because she had an order of deportation before she got married she was not eligible for a resident visa. The case is that Hispanics or those from any other country, should know that the law is the law and we can misinterpret the law or claim separation of the family that actually is being done by the parents, but we have to respect the law and that is final. About separation of the family, and I interpret my life, when we come to this country legally we also undergo separation of the family and when the children are small, I feel they should be raised by the mother. To leave the children with another family does not speak well of the parents.

The next concern is what is related by the television news. For example, when we talk about solving problems, can we see that the worst group is the Hispanic? We have to realize that there is a concern for what happens when they come here. For example, in obesity, we have the highest percentage of adults and children. However, many of these obese adults will develop diabetes mellitus with its complications, mainly hypertension. When we speak about HIV and hepatitis C, Hispanic immigrants have the highest rates of infected population. When we talk about immunizations, the Hispanics are the ones who ignore the law. I have seen during the past two weeks about five adolescents. When asking about the vaccination against HPV, they all knew very briefly what the vaccination cured, but no one got the medication. When we see the pregnant adolescents, Hispanics have the highest incidence. There was a report that the children of grade schools do not go to classes for more than 20 days; however, the highest percentage is Hispanics. Why all these changes when the Hispanic immigrants stay in the United States has to be investigated.

As previously stated, this manuscript is for the understanding by the Hispanic immigrants who live in the United States, the numbers now reaching the level of the developed country. It is difficult to make a future without having a high school diploma, preferably college, or another profession. The people who are planning to come to this country should be aware that the life is not as many years before, it is very expensive and any person who comes with the idea of improving their future and does not have an education will suffer more than if they remain in their home country. On the other hand, college in the Hispanic countries is considerably cheaper than the United States, and the only thing one needs is a good brain and/or motivation. These people who are planning to come to the United States will know about the expensive life.

The people who are already in the United States also should be aware they can have a better life back in their home country and not to try to live out of welfare or the US government.

For the group of the undocumented, illegal residents, I would have to repeat what Dr. Nancy Alvares already said, "Go back to your country and if you do not have a criminal record get your papers properly approved by the Immigration Department and come back legally." This is the best advice I can give to this group.

As you can see, all of the above problems, plus the ones that I described; integration, language barrier, and discrimination will make it very difficult to live a good life in this country.

As a final comment, as I outlined in the introduction, it is very difficult to live in this country, mainly at the present time when the cost of living is high and almost compatible with the other developed countries. It is not my intention to discourage immigration to the United States, but my recommendation is that it should be properly planned with the approval of the immigration at their respective embassies. Consider the lack of employment due to the economical crisis.

CHAPTER 9
ADMISSION OF IGNORANCE OR MISTAKE IS THE BEGINNING OF WISDOM

It is important to admit mistakes, mainly when they are obvious. However, this does not happen with Hispanics. They can defend their mistakes; even when there is no way to do it otherwise. There is an expression in Mexico, actually in Jalisco that says, "Jalisco never loses and when they lose they rebate."

The above happens many times when there are obvious mistakes in coming to this country. People realize they are going to be better off if they go back to their own country, but they will never admit that they made a mistake and go back to restart again. When they come to the United States they sell everything or give it away, but they usually come with very little possessions thinking in this country they are going to find clothes, furniture, and money. With the current economical situation, few people are going back. Of course, after they use credit cards to take advantage of all the credit, then they leave. The majority will wait with the false expectation that the crisis is going to get better. They are jobless and literally they do not have money to pay their commitments, such as cars, houses, etc. They do not realize that the activists and television give the expectation of the false impression this is going to be a recession that is going to last a short time as they have a new president who is the salvation for United States and the world. It is time for Hispanics to go back, and I feel this economical crisis will not recover, even after four years, with the controversial errors of our new president. For example, knowing how prisons are because I spent

16 months working and observing these institutions, the closure of the Guantanamo prison is a big mistake unless they are going to have a special place in the United States to harbor all these terrorists. Otherwise, the people who are incarcerated in Guantanamo are going to corrupt other prisoners, and the terrorism is going to expand instead of disappear. Hispanics, please do not harm your family, your children, and even yourself, thinking the economical crisis is not going to last long. Even after recovery of this crisis, the high cost of living will not be for persons without a higher level of education, a good understanding of the English language, and integration to society.

The hopes placed on President Obama are not going to happen as Hispanics thought when they changed their vote for reform of immigration laws. Speaking about President Obama, one should know that his presidency is now complicated. The economical crisis has been approached by unusual methods. For example, giving money to industrial companies such as General Motors and Chrysler was not a good idea as now they are asking for more money or perhaps face bankruptcy. Many times it is better to construct a new building than repair the old ones that are filled with insects and disease. If Mr. Obama placed the money in an institution that was new from the beginning just to help the people this probably was the best approach to the initial economic crisis. Now he sees that the world also has their hopes in him. Recently European countries welcomed him, but no one wants to follow his ideas. He has significant problems with the Congress and he also has created problems with Cuba and other countries. Perhaps President Obama needs an advisor who will not agree with anything offered to unless it is what they want. The people who voted for him within the Hispanic group are very unhappy because despite the economic crisis they request immigration reform. During television activities' programs (Jorge Ramos, who in his special program, Al Punto, To The Point), the question always comes up about when immigration reform is going to occur. On the other hand, Obama's popularity is coming down from 78 %to less than 50%. Another way of looking at the facts is that being a minority president in moment of an economical crisis without experience, as was voiced during the campaign, he will have to face more than he can handle. It is my impression that his popularity will continue going down, not because he is not a good president but because of the problems he is currently facing. He will not have time to attend to all of them, and immigration reform is one to go by the wayside.

This book is not intended to display the usual life of the immigrants, but to make them aware that coming to this country is getting too difficult. As Dr. Nancy Alvares says, especially directed to the undocumented immigrant, "it is better for them to return to their countries and once they have their papers ready to come legally." Still in that situation, they have to face the high cost of living, mainly in this current period of recession.

As it was previously outlined, the three difficulties that immigrants face in this country are language barrier, integration, and discrimination. Of these three difficult situations, the one that is almost impossible to achieve is integration. Latin Americans want to come to this country and continue their life as before, ignoring the laws and living conditions. Of course, the language barrier is almost impossible to overcome as we will never speak like an

American, and with the television stations presenting wonderful programs we are mostly watching Spanish television stations and ignoring the English language. On the other hand, the accent is most difficult for Hispanic immigrants. Discrimination is another difficult problem. There also activists in foreign countries, such as the case of Arellano, who did the impossible trying to stay in this country. After reentrance to this country she was deported and she decided to go to a Christian church to serve as a sanctuary. In the end, this situation did not work and she was deported and now she is an activist in Mexico. She has a good life, she is a prominent person, and she encourages people to disobey the laws and come to this country without thinking they are sending these immigrants to what I call hell in heaven.

While I was preparing this book the American presidential elections were held. Hispanics in the previous elections were in favor of Mr. Bush, who they thought was going to help immigrants with what they mostly requested— reform of immigration laws. Contrary to that, Mr. Bush decided to establish laws to capture immigrants who were already convicted of crimes and then the activists were criticizing the President. They practically decided the election of Mr. Bush four years ago. At this time they thought the election of Senator Obama was going to be their salvation because he is a black man. However, it is my feeling this it is impossible for a president to break immigration laws. If they consider illegal immigrants for citizenship, they will probably do it with restrictions that in the end only about 10 to 15% will be eligible for citizenship or residency. Mr. Obama received the majority of votes from the Hispanic immigrants, and he will have to attend to the economic crisis and perhaps in the far future he will try to make some immigration reform changes.

So what is behind the request to legalize the 12 to 15 million undocumented immigrants? By talking to people and searching within the Hispanic population I found out they are hopeful and encouraged by the activists that the US will have a president of Hispanic origin in the near future and at that time the laws are going to be dictated by the Hispanic population. The problem with this group of immigrants is that they do not request or ask for reform, but they try to demand changes in the immigration laws. Hispanic immigrants do not realize the present crisis began with the problems of real estate that show inflation of sales of the properties with resultant foreclosures. Now comes the acquisition of cars, which they cannot pay for.

Next, the difficulty the government has is mostly secondary to the Hispanic immigration that purchased houses at inflated or super inflated prices.

I can go on and on how immigrants with no profession will not achieve success economically in this country. To survive in this country, the most needed professions are doctors, nurses, dentists, architects and possibly computer technicians. Otherwise, be aware that the majority of immigrants, especially women, are serving as housekeepers, abused by their employers.

As a final remark, I would like to say to the potential immigrants, assess first the problems that I have described above and then with that knowledge come with the idea of beginning a new life. This is not heaven as it looks. Perhaps Americans are really enjoying this country that is the best country in the world. I myself have to say I came to this country trying to get out of the poverty and to avoid the path of my family, but the situations I went through were not very pleasant. I went through the period of language barrier, I had problems integrating to the life in this country, and I was thoroughly discriminated against— Dr. Arana cannot be recommended because he is foreign born and foreign trained...

Hispanics, assess your situation and as I mentioned above, be aware of the future problems without thinking that the economical crisis will end shortly. Recognize that you made a mistake coming to this country and go back to your own places and try to initiate a life with your friends, relatives, and on your own soil. Don't do what I did because I was pushed by a situation that I could not overcome, to follow the path of my family, and that was the main reason why I remained in this country, but I was aware of what was going to happen and that economically I was not going to suffer, even in a crisis like the current one.

While I was finishing the work on this manuscript, on 1/27/2009, I heard in the news of Univision station that two minors went on a hunger strike because their mother is being sent to Nicaragua. The story began sometime ago when the parents of these children received deportation orders. They ignored the notice, and the mother was apprehended by the Immigration on 12/19/2008 and placed in a detention center. Children went on a hunger strike. To my understanding, this is a crime because of the horrendous psychological trauma that these children are going through, and that is being applauded by the television stations as heroic behavior. I do not believe children should be harmed with these psychological conditions, and this is more than the physical trauma of not eating. The mother was deported by 1/28/2009. Another more painful news story was the Hispanic who, along with his wife, was removed from his job in a hospital. He came home, killed his five children and his wife, and then committed suicide. I do not think Hispanics understand the law is the law, and now we are going through an economical crisis that is not going to be short term, but who knows, 3 to 5 years from now, the life in this country will be at the level of the other developed countries. Now my question is, "is it worth it to go through this pain and suffering because we do not return to our country to live with our people and to have a better life?" My answer is, this is beyond my imagination.

When I arrived to this country I thought I was coming to heaven and when I opened my eyes I was in hell. The name of this book is the most appropriate for this problem. I encountered myself what I call hell in spite of being in heaven.

CHAPTER 10
FINAL COMMENTS

For the benefit of the readers, I would like to discus important issues and information that was previously mentioned, but briefly.

Separation of the Family: This issue has been publicized widely by Hispanic newspapers, television, radio announcers, politicians, and others. When one of the parents or both are deported and sent to their countries, the children born in the United States can remain in this country. This situation is then blamed on the United States, as a terrible mistake. What we do not understand and those who do understand, try to ignore, that this is a country of laws and to coming here without documents brings a chance of being separated from their kids. Of course, children are not prepared for this situation, which is a mistake of the parents. When this happens, the proper conduct is to return to their country with their children. The case of Elvira Arellano terminated this proper way.

On the other hand, I do not appreciate that people like Christina, as she presented on her show on October 17, 2009, cases of families that were partially or totally separated from their parents. To obtain credit from the human pain is not written in my brain. She also exposed some undocumented children to a national TV audience. Thank you, Christina.

The Case of Lou Dobbs: This television program dedicated a great deal of time in talking about the illegal or undocumented immigrants. From time to time, I listen to this program. Please understand Mr. Dobbs is just protecting his country, and you, by pointing out that a massive number of the undocumented aliens will lead to increased numbers of uneducated populations, which eventually will account for the longer economical crisis. Their production is much less than their expenditure. Of course, with all the propaganda, Hispanics become more sensitive and defensive like what I saw on Univision when Ana Maria Canseco said that she was not happy because the immigration wrote on her admission card "Legal Immigrant." For the happiness of the complainers, Lou Dobbs has just resigned from his program on CNN as of November 10, 2009.

Hispanics of middle and lower class can be educated better in their countries of origin, and then they can obtain legal entrance to this country after they finish their college education. I, myself, come from a lower class in Peru, and it was easier for me to obtain a medical degree in Peru, with high honors from a government medical school, which was inexpensive.

The Art of Making a Request : What Hispanics do not learn is how to make a request. On the contrary, we demand for illegal requisitions. To make legal citizens out of undocumented immigrants who broke the law is to have to change the law. When this situation happens, it is better not to demand the change. As Maria Celeste and Maria Marin discussed in their program "Al Rojo Vivo," on October 21, 2009, we have to be nice and generally, we have to know how to ask for things or to ask for something out of the ordinary.

This is a different country and a different culture and if we want to live with Americans, we have to change, not to continue with what is otherwise normal for us.

Our president is of the minority population, and perhaps he made too many promises he couldn't keep, as he was anxious to write history in the United States. Or, he was inexperienced and offered what he could not accomplish. The name of the game is not to ask what the country can do for us but what we can do for the country, as per our past president John F. Kennedy. Let's work for America. Remember that the world is increasing in violence, assaults, ignorance, drug addiction, venereal diseases and, generally, in crime and ignorance. Hispanics, let's change gears and increase our education and our desires to work and succeed. Learn English and walk with your chin up.

Now, as a brother born and raised in Peru, I would like to express my thoughts and opinions about the manuscript. Although it looks like the content of the manuscript favors Americans, my intention is for you to understand that the truth is different.

Activists, television and radio announcers, politicians, and even artists encourage you to stay in this country, where they have a wonderful life and they make good money. They do this because of your presence. Having more Hispanics in this country will give them more power, and you will be the ones who will suffer the poverty, the humiliation to obtain food, foreclosures on your residences, and unemployment. Your children will have to interrupt their schooling to work for your family's survival or they will join gangs to assault, rob, and even murder, sometimes against your own people, just to exist here. Your female relatives who work in the fields are subject to sexual abuse as described by Cristina Londonio in her documentary shown on Telemundo News on November 10, 2009. In addition, many children will become prostitutes to earn money to survive which, in general, leads to disaster. In school, 40% of the students won't finish high school, and several will become pregnant. The greatest incidence of HIV, Hepatitis C, diabetes and obesity, and venereal disease is among the Hispanic population. Is it worth it to go through all of the above just for the pleasure of living in this country? My answer is no. Remember that every time we recognize that we're wrong, we are learning something that was unknown to us.

In case that Hispanics become a majority population and they elect a Latin American as a President of the United States, that person will change the laws; however, they would be the same laws and ways of life as when you left your country of origin. Politicians will rule the country and the population will be of secondary importance. On the other hand, remember the episode when our past president Bill Clinton went to North Korea to ask for the liberation of the journalists who were indicted and convicted? The Koreans did not argue, and the two journalists came back to the United States without any problems. However, when Michelle and Barack Obama went to the Olympic committee to campaign for the city of Chicago, that was the first city eliminated. These stories remind me that the Caucasian American is more respected abroad and here in the United States and it will most likely be a long time for minorities to obtain power and respect that many white Americans do. Although this episode constitutes an act of discrimination, it is true and will happen for many more years to come. On the other hand, we Hispanics complain when we are not well and when we are well. That attitude does not apply to this country. On May 1, 2007, there was a case of police brutality in Los Angeles where the police abused their authority against Hispanics. This case was recently dismissed, but it was about the police targeting Hispanics in what was a peaceful rally in the park.

Another episode was when a lady who has been a resident since 1980 was stopped because of an illegal U-turn. In the interaction with police, she was also given a citation because she didn't speak English and now she wants to make a complaint for her suffering during what she said was this illegal procedure. How many times has she had to suffer for not speaking the language? When you look at it, the chances of her speaking English, after thirty years in this country, is slim to none.

In another instance, multiple complaints made against a now famous Sheriff Arpaio didn't stop him from his activities of arresting illegal immigrants. Instead he was given more money to continue his activities. However, complaints to remove Lou Dodds from CNN for the way he conducts his program, mostly against illegal immigrants, will not be heard. The same will happen with the complaints being prepared by Anna Munoz, a law student in Washington, D.C., who defends the rights of the undocumented immigrants. They will not progress. As I referred to in a prior chapter of this book, it is a fact that discrimination in this country as I have noticed in almost every country that I have visited, especially when we are in competition. This is why President Obama is not as popular as he once was, as would be any minority who is elected president of this country. Recent elections on November 3, 2009, revealed that his popularity is declining as his party lost major campaigns in Virginia and New Jersey, where in the presidential election, he won by an overwhelming majority.

In my situation, it was unquestionably an act of discrimination when the Chief of Surgery wrote the adverse letter against me and it was only because I was competing with him. However, instead of complaining, I kept on demonstrating to my patients, my family, and myself that I was a good surgeon.

Brother Hispanics, have in mind that to survive in this country, a college education and proficient knowledge of the English language are essential for survival. I will close this chapter with the recommendations of the attorney Ana Maria Polo of the show Caso Cerrado on Telemundo: "Obtain the most education possible, walk correctly, respect others to obtain respect for yourself and I add my own recommendation; always tell the truth as a good example to your own children."

Always remember, it appears that we come to HEAVEN; however, when we wake up, we realize the American Dream is rather a nightmare, and thus, we are in HELL.